T0149454

CHENNAI
from an
AMERICAN'S
PERSPECTIVE

CHENNAI
from an
AMERICAN'S
PERSPECTIVE

PAUL BOUCHARD

CHENNAI FROM AN AMERICAN'S PERSPECTIVE

iUniverse books may be ordered through booksellers or by contacting:

iUniverse
1663 Liberty Drive
Bloomington, IN 47403
www.iuniverse.com
1-800-Authors (1-800-288-4677)

ISBN: 978-1-5320-3261-5 (sc)
ISBN: 978-1-5320-3260-8 (e)

Library of Congress Control Number: 2017915946

Print information available on the last page.

iUniverse rev. date: 11/13/2017

I finally visited India, specifically Chennai, India, the city of my wife's birth, during the last week of 2016.

My wife made the necessary hotel and airline reservations and visa applications, and I completed the mandatory military foreign travel packet. Everything was set to go, but then, out of nowhere, a perfect storm of four phenomena was brewing, damping our hopes yet again of visiting India. First, a key high-level Chennai politician was dying, and one of my sisters-in-law who lives in Chennai (I have five sisters-in-law, two of whom live in Chennai with my mother-in-law) informed my wife and I that if this politician passed away, most of Chennai would shut down for a day or two for proper mourning.

Second, a major cyclone had recently hit Chennai, causing a lot of debris and disruptions. Third, currency limits were imposed on everyone in India, including tourists, the daily withdrawal limit being set at no more than the equivalent of seventy-five American dollars in rupees, the Indian currency. And fourth, employees of British Airways, the airline we had booked our tickets with, were threatening to go on strike Christmas Day.

Figures, I thought. *Now just ain't the right time to visit Chennai. My wife has visited Chennai numerous times since we got married in 2004, but never with me. Will I ever visit India?*

Then the tide of events changed in our favor. The city of Chennai was cleaning up, and the forecast called for clear weather; no cyclones were on the radar screen. Then the politician's health miraculously turned around. The currency situation—specifically limiting certain bills as a means to curb corruption—stayed in full force, but my wife kept monitoring the situation, and her research showed tourists managing their affairs by using credit cards where allowed and asking merchants, particularly hotel management, to run up food and beverage tabs so they could pay in full at the end of their stay.

My biggest concern, however, was the threatened British Airways strike - that would really mess up our vacation plans. I gave serious thought to getting a partial refund and booking with another airline, but my wife kept visiting the British Airways website, and the airline insisted they would honor their commitments, and should a strike occur, they'd arrange other flights for customers.

With that, we boarded British Airways at Dulles Airport outside Washington, DC, the evening of December 23. The first stop was London, with a seven-hour layover at Heathrow Airport. Next stop, Chennai.

We arrived at Chennai Airport in the early hours of Christmas Day. The airport was quiet and modern. The tile floors were clean and polished, and I couldn't help but notice the large, intricate wood carvings, mostly of Hindu gods, that populated the walls. I also couldn't help but notice the damp, heavy air and the lack of air-conditioning.

My wife, who had experienced that airport many times during her visits to Chennai, was behind me, dragging her wheeled luggage. (Our luggage had arrived at the baggage claim on time without incident.) She said, "Brace yourself. Going through immigration will take some time." Sure enough, a long line was forming at the immigration counter, and customs officers were nowhere to be seen.

After about fifteen minutes of waiting, two men, neatly dressed in cream-colored uniforms consisting of collared shirts and pressed pants, took their seats behind raised desks. Leading up to the raised desks were two metal steps. All the travelers had to climb the two steps and show their visas and get their passports stamped. In front of the customs officers, on a raised countertop, were small machines that resembled credit card processors. As I inched my way toward the customs desks while the line slowly move forward, I noticed travelers placing their fingers on the machine for scanning. I also saw a sign behind one of the customs officers that read, "Senior Citizens and Differently Abled."

Differently abled, not disabled, I thought. *I guess Indians are more politically correct then we Americans are.* The sign was ignored, however; regardless of age or ability, travelers went to either one of the two desks as their turn came up.

It took us about thirty minutes to get to the front of the line as passports were slowly being stamped. My wife was standing next to me just in case her assistance was needed. (An American citizen since 2009 and a former Indian citizen, she had a ten-year visa that would be processed at a different station.)

Suddenly, at the customs desk to the right, I heard the customs officer say, "No, no. Forefinger. Forefinger." The woman standing on the top step was struggling with the device. She was a middle-aged British woman with whom my wife and I had briefly spoken to earlier. I could see she kept placing one finger on the small machine to the frustration of the customs officer.

Finally, the officer raised his hand in front of her, his palm facing her, with his thumb bent inside so he was displaying four fingers. The woman needed to scan four fingers, but the customs officer had said *forefinger* instead of the plural *four fingers*, and she had kept placing her index finger on the machine.

Language barriers, I thought. *Interesting.*

"Next," said the other customs officer. I moved up to the desk, climbed the steps, and promised myself I'd complete the finger-scanning drill without fault. I handed my passport and visa to the customs officer.

"Whose address is this on your visa?" he asked politely

as he looked at my documents. I gestured for my wife to move forward next to me, just below the steps, and said, "My mother-in-law's, sir. My wife's mother."

"Oh, I see," he said.

Then we went through the finger-scanning drill without any hiccups, and he stamped my passport.

My wife and I walked to the right to get in line for her visa processing at another station, and as we walked by, we noticed the British woman, still at the customs desk, now sitting on one of the metal steps, looking faint. Her son and husband were standing next to her, and the son asked for a bag, fearing his mom might vomit. My wife and I moved on, feeling bad for her.

As we were walking, my wife said, "Processing my passport shouldn't take too long. And then we need to go to the currency exchange desk to get as many rupees as we can."

My wife's passport was processed in no time, and we got in line at the currency exchange station. The line was moving at a snail's pace. A middle-aged couple with three young daughters was behind us, and we engaged in polite conversation. They were from Belgium, they informed us, and were visiting India to relax and practice yoga.

Our turn came up. Behind a see-through Plexiglas wall was a man dressed in dark pants, a white shirt, and a blue vest. To his right was a young woman, similarly dressed, except she wore a long skirt instead of pants. To the man's left was a copying machine. I let my wife handle our currency exchange needs.

"How much money can we exchange, sir?" she asked the man. "We have US dollars."

"Seventy-five dollars per person," the man said.

"What is the exchange rate?" my wife asked.

"Sixty-three rupees per dollar."

"And that's all? Only seventy-five dollars?" my wife said, a bit frustrated.

"No. You can also put a maximum of fifty thousand rupees on a prepaid credit card."

We elected to get as many rupees as we could, so we both put money on prepaid credit cards. Frustratingly, the process of getting money was slow and bureaucratic: papers to print, then sign, then copying again, then generating a credit card and filling out more paperwork, then generating pin numbers for the credit cards.

More travelers were standing in the currency exchange line, and everyone seemed frustrated that the line wasn't moving. One man, who I presumed was British by the way he spoke, simply gave up and exited the line, saying, "And they call India an emerging market. This is ridiculous."

Finally the man behind the Plexiglas gave us the rupees in cash and the two prepaid credit cards. With that, my wife and I followed the exit signs out of the airport, which read, "Way Out" instead of "Exit."

In five minutes, we were outside the airport. The sun was bright, and I figured the temperature was in the eighties with high humidity. My wife saw one of her sisters and a niece waving in our direction, and in no time we were exchanging greetings. My wife's sister also gave us a beautiful flower arrangement.

"Come, come," the sister said. "We'll get a taxi."

We walked with our luggage in tow for no more than two hundred feet then selected the first taxi from a line of taxis. The taxis were very old and black with yellow tops. They reminded me of American taxis from the 1950s, the type still running in Cuba. I noticed some motorcycles and motor scooters, and small three-wheeled, open-seated vehicles that were more carts than cars. Above us was a long concrete overpass.

The cabdriver was young and polite, and he placed our luggage in the trunk of his old taxi. I got in the back seat with my wife and niece while my sister-in-law sat in the front passenger seat to the driver's left, given that the steering wheel was on the right side.

I pulled at the seatbelt to buckle up, but the strap wouldn't come loose. "Honey," I said to my wife. "My seatbelt doesn't seem to work."

She smiled and said, "Most seatbelts don't work."

The cabdriver turned to face me and said, "No seatbelt."

Sweet, I thought.

He placed the car in gear and started driving. As the taxi pulled onto a street, we entered complete and utter chaos: small cars surrounded by tons of motorcycles, motor scooters, and three-wheeled motorized carts. There were no painted dividing lines on the roads to organize traffic, and all vehicles were driving on the left side, with no more than a foot separating each vehicle from the other. Motorcycles and motor scooters were weaving and zipping by slower traffic. To my amazement, some of the motorcycles held three or four passengers, with a small child sitting on the gas tank, followed by the motorcycle driver, followed by a child or a woman carrying an infant. And few passengers wore helmets.

I also couldn't help but notice that women drove a good number of the motor scooters, and all women—whether pedestrians or vehicle passengers or motor scooter drivers— wore colorful saris or the traditional dress pants and shirt called *salwar kameez*. I also noticed that female passengers always sat in a sidesaddle position on motorcycles, never with the seat between their legs.

The traffic was bustling, and our taxi started speeding up. I thought, *This isn't good. We're going to get into an accident.* I imagined the following as a true possibility:

> My company commander to my battalion commander: "Sir, I regret to inform you I have some bad news. Major Bouchard died in a car accident during his Christmas vacation in India."

> Battalion commander: "Christ, that's bad. Well, you know the drill. We have rules and regulations for these unfortunate events. Contact the Red Cross so they can notify the family and next of kin. Call the embassy, and arrange for the body to be flown back to the States. And, as you know, we'll have to do a LODI [line of duty investigation]. The investigating officer

has to be a higher rank than the deceased, so appoint a lieutenant colonel."

Company commander: "Yes, sir. On it, sir. We'll get a LODI going right away."

Battalion commander: "Now let's cut to the chase. Do we know if Bouchard was at fault?"

Company commander: "Well, sir, the Chennai police department report says he was a passenger in a taxi, but he wasn't wearing a seatbelt. Apparently, the seatbelt wasn't working."

Battalion commander: "Well then, Bouchard should have never gotten into that taxi. Christ, he really screwed the pooch on this one. The investigative officer will have to find Not in the Line of Duty Due to Soldier's Misconduct. With that, I think Bouchard's beneficiaries won't be entitled to his group life insurance proceeds. Hell, we do all these safety briefs, but look what happened in this case. This will serve as a good lesson for all our soldiers. Captain, be sure to put some PowerPoint slides together on this case once the LODI is closed. We'll use this as a case study for our Safety First campaign for the entire battalion at our quarterly town hall meeting."

I really thought we'd get into an accident. Traffic wasn't

moving too fast, but fast enough, and every vehicle—be it a small car, motorcycle, motor scooter, or three-wheeled cart—was very close to other vehicles. I looked at the passengers and drivers in the other vehicles, and none of them were wearing seatbelts. *Madness*, I thought.

The traffic kept moving without incident, and I realized I couldn't control the situation, so I might as well try to relax and not worry. I decided to observe the surroundings as our taxi kept navigating the traffic: some decent roads, but most of them with no painted dividing lines; many, many buildings, most of them old, with a sprinkle of some newer modern-looking ones; some streets with sidewalks, but some without; many people walking in the streets; some pedestrians talking on cell phones; all women wearing saris or the traditional salwar kameez—no jeans, no shorts, no T-shirts; men dressed in pants and often short-sleeve shirts, but some in loose-fitting, cream-colored pants and long-sleeve shirts reaching down nearly to their knees; all the drivers of motorcycles were men while many of the motor scooter drivers were women, and only about half of all these drivers wore helmets. The pedestrians mostly wore sandals, with the rest wearing shoes or going barefoot. And almost everyone was Indian; I saw no Westerners, no foreigners. I did see some beggars, and I noticed they were always older and always sitting on the sidewalks, their legs crossed Indian style. I didn't see any begging children.

Our taxi kept driving along, maneuvering around the jammed traffic. Suddenly I started hearing horns from all directions. I guess I had tuned out those sounds, being amazed at the traffic and how close the vehicles were to each other. But as I relaxed, I noticed the constant beep, beep, beep of vehicle horns. It seemed honking one's horn was the key to keeping the traffic moving, and I began to notice patterns to the honking. One short beep or two short beeps from a driver seemed to mean *I'm here and I'm coming through*. Three short beeps seemed to mean *I'm coming through faster*. And the long-held beeeeeeeep meant *Get out of the way*.

Our taxi came to a sudden stop, and I wondered why. I peered through the front windshield and noticed three goats crossing the street. Once the goats were safely on the sidewalk, the traffic and the beeping resumed.

Our taxi pulled into the circular driveway of our hotel. Before we reached the main entrance, a mustachioed guard, dressed in what looked like a police officer's uniform, raised his hand, the signal for the taxi to stop. I noticed the driver pulling a lever to release the trunk hatch, and then I noticed another guard stepping in front of the taxi. That guard was carrying a stick resembling a long broom handle, and at the bottom of the stick was a wide mirror. He placed the stick directly perpendicular to the cab's hood, and he peered down. I knew exactly what he was doing: checking the taxi's underside while the second guard checked the trunk. They were both checking for car bombs. India has had its share of terrorist attacks, so security, where necessary, is tight. An upscale hotel like ours could be such a target.

I heard our trunk close, and the front guard waved us forward.

We got our luggage, thanked and paid the cab driver, and immediately were greeted by two of the hotel's bellhops. They were dressed in neat cream-colored uniforms with wide red belts. They greeted us by saying, "Good afternoon," as they placed their right arms at a forty-five-degree angle, their right hands over their hearts, and gave the slightest quick forward nod of their heads. To the left was a conveyor belt with a U-shaped scanner on top of it. My wife, who always stayed at this hotel during her visits to Chennai, knew the drill. The scanner checked luggage for bombs, weapons, and contraband.

Our luggage was scanned, and we entered the hotel. It was beautiful, with polished tile floors, marble columns, and intricately detailed crown molding. To the right was a glass case filled with beautiful cakes, and to the left was the concierge's desk and a large beautiful sofa. And directly in front of us, blocking our view of the main desk area, was a gorgeous artificial Christmas tree standing at least twenty feet tall.

We checked in, took the elevator to our room, unpacked, showered, and put on our clothes. My niece helped us figure out how to set the air-conditioning to our liking and how to work the flat-screen television. Our hotel room was comparable to a nice, slightly upscale American hotel. I looked outside and noticed a beautiful swimming pool on the ground floor. I then took a few photos of the city.

It was sunny and hot out, and the city air was hazy. I noticed most buildings were white. In the distance, I saw a mosque and a couple of temples. I also realized that Chennai truly is a very large city.

We called for another cab, got in (it didn't have any functioning seat belts either), and in forty minutes we were at my mother-in-law's house. Jammed traffic and beeping horns were now familiar to me, so this drive didn't have any shock effect.

My mother-in-law's home is a gated square building in the middle of a narrow street surrounded by similar buildings. We got our luggage out of the taxi, paid the driver, and headed inside the house, where my mother-in-law and my wife's oldest sister greeted us. This sister had a big smile, and she was holding a golden plate that had a short flame in it. She started making circles with the plate.

"Hello, Paul," she said. "This is a traditional Indian greeting. The flame gives good energy."

I smiled and said hello to both my sister-in-law and my mother-in-law. My wife and I removed our shoes and entered the house. Immediately we were in a large, high-ceilinged living room with a nice tile floor. Two couches and three chairs lined the room. There were two bedrooms to the right of the living room and a dining room to the left, next to the kitchen. There was also a small bedroom to the left of the living room. My wife and I sat down, engaged in conversation, and took photos.

In less than an hour, we were served lunch, which

consisted of grilled fish with rice. My wife and mother-in-
law both eat fish, but my two sisters-in-law and my niece are
strict vegetarians.

After lunch, the younger sister-in-law showed me the
small bedroom to the left of the entranceway. She explained to
me that this was the *puja*, or prayer room. "Every home has a
puja, Paul, and it's always in the northeast corner of the house,
where the sun is the strongest. The apartments upstairs have
pujas too." She then explained the basic tenets of Hinduism,
one of the world's oldest religions and philosophies. Her
explanation was interesting, and I thanked her for describing
the importance of energy and personal development, how
Hindus invented the number zero, and how gods can have
avatars—that is, different manifestations. The room had
displays of different gods and various plates with different
incense sticks. It was a nice, quiet, peaceful room.

Around one o'clock in the afternoon, I felt very tired—
jet lag was no doubt setting in—so I took a nap in one of
the bedrooms. What I thought would be a two-hour nap
turned into five hours of solid sleep. My wife woke me up
and suggested it was best to head to our hotel. It was six and
already dark outside.

Minutes later, a taxi showed up at the house, and my wife
and I got in it. Traffic was heavy, but not as bad as the morning
ride from the airport. Vehicle horns were still honking with
their ever-present beeps, and most roads didn't have dividing
lines. There were streetlights, but I felt more were needed. I

noticed pedestrians walking the streets, talking on their cell phones.

Then, out of nowhere, I saw a brown cow crossing the road, vehicles gingerly passing around it.

It was building after building after building and street after street after street. Occasionally, we'd come to a traffic circle, and motorcycles, motor scooters, and small cars traveled only a couple of feet from our small taxi. But there were no accidents; traffic moved along. Thank God, for again I wasn't wearing a seatbelt.

We got to our room, and I immediately reached inside the small fridge and pulled out one of the two bottles of the British Empire brand beer. I had never heard of—let alone tasted—this beer. I changed into shorts and a T-shirt, and I made a small toast to Chennai and India.

"Merry Christmas," I told my wife.

"Merry Christmas, Paulie," she said.

"To Chennai, India," I said.

"To Chennai, India."

I drank the beer and slept soundly.

Day two of our vacation consisted of shopping and spending time at my mother-in-law's house. The day began with a large breakfast buffet in the hotel's restaurant, consisting of both traditional Western and Indian breakfast items. I had croissants, bacon, chicken sausages, and an omelet, and my wife and I shared a *dosa*, a rice crepe filled with potatoes. The only American breakfast items I didn't see were pancakes and waffles. Sinatra music was playing, and I couldn't help but notice references to London and America on the walls: an Elvis poster, London street names, and a poster of the movie *Casablanca* with Humphrey Bogart prominently displayed.

The wait staff was very attentive, and they continuously gave us the greeting of a crossed right arm over the chest and slight nod. It was a lovely breakfast, and it catered, in part, to Westerners. But I saw none; everyone at the large buffet room was Indian. I wanted to tip the staff, but my wife said, "No, there's no tipping here." I also saw that other patrons weren't tipping, so no tipping it was.

After breakfast, we exited the hotel, and waiting for us were my niece and a driver in a small car. There's a bit of a story here: My wife's family is part of the second-highest cast (there are four main castes in Hinduism), which means they are middle class, which also means they own a car. The previous day I hadn't noticed the car at my mother-in-law's home, but now, there it was, parked at the hotel's front entrance.

Our driver's name was Rajesh, a young man of medium height who looked to be in his mid- to late twenties. My mother-in-law and my two sisters-in-law and niece all live together, and they own this car. But none of them know how to drive it, which explains the need to hire a driver like Rajesh. Rajesh was not a personal driver for my wife's family; rather, he worked for a driving company. But my sisters-in-law knew Rajesh personally, and we were informed we had his services for the duration of our short vacation.

The small white car was a Suzuki sedan with five-speed manual transmission. Rajesh got into the driver's seat, and I decided to sit in the front seat next to him. Right away, I couldn't believe my good fortune: my seatbelt was functional. *Yes!* I snapped it on and thought, *Line of duty investigations won't be necessary now.* Rajesh started the car, and we pulled out of the hotel. Our destination was a gift shop my wife wanted to visit.

The streets were packed with vehicles: small cars, small trucks, motorcycles and motor scooters, and three-wheeled vehicles, which my niece informed me are called—what else?—autos. Relaxed and focused, I now noticed the makes of the motorcycles: Honda, Suzuki, and Royal Enfield, a local brand. We drove by a Harley-Davidson dealership, but I didn't notice any Harleys on the streets. The cars were mostly Suzukis, Hyundais, Tatas, and Volkswagens, with a sprinkle of Hondas and Fords. I couldn't make out the motor scooter brands; they all looked alike.

The perpetual beep, beep, beep of horns could be heard everywhere. And the sites were just like the day before: many pedestrians wearing sandals while other pedestrians walking barefoot or with shoes; all the women wearing saris or the traditional chemise and loose-fitting pants—no shorts and no jeans.

There were numerous buildings, and many of them had black mildew next to the rooftops. Some of the remnants of the cyclone that had hit Chennai the previous week were still present: debris and twigs and downed trees. I often saw older women bent down, sweeping the sidewalks, their brooms not a long stick with a plank filled with stiff bristles like the ones at big-box stores, but rather a bunch of thin twigs.

Suddenly I noticed a man, well dressed in beige pants and a white shirt, standing in front of a building. I couldn't believe what I was seeing: he was urinating with vehicles passing and pedestrians walking by as if it was no big deal. I thought, *In the United States, a police officer would give this man a citation, but here, who knows?* Nobody seemed to notice. Everybody just kept walking, minding their won business. No one arrested or even confronted him.

Rajesh kept navigating the Chennai streets, shifting the transmission when necessary, and hardly using the turn signal. Like the other drivers, he used the horn liberally, tapping it— beep, beep, beep—what seemed to be every twenty seconds. As I looked at him engaged in his trade, I noticed he had removed his sandals; he was driving barefoot.

I kept observing things as we made our way through traffic: the occasional cow on the side of the road, and dogs here and there, either trotting about or simply lying down, absorbing the sun's rays. None of the dogs had leashes or owners; they were all strays with no one stopping to feed them or pet them.

Occasionally I saw a traffic cop in the middle of the street, blowing his whistle, directing traffic with hand and arm movements. Surprisingly, given the sheer volume of vehicles on the streets and how close they were to each other, I had seen no accidents—not one.

I started taking photos with my cell phone: yield signs were identical to ours in the States, but the word "Yield" was not present; instead was the phrase "Make Way." I noticed restaurants and a fair number of ice cream parlors, but no bars; stores of all types were present, such as hardware stores, jewelry stores, and fashion stores. I noticed a few gyms and medical clinics. And on the large concrete fence or wall that lined a particular street, posters of politicians, religious leaders, and actors were plastered. Occasionally I saw women dressed entirely in black with most of their heads covered, though their faces were visible. "Honey," I said to my wife. "I take it the ladies I see dressed in black are Muslims."

"That's correct," she replied. Then my niece, a recent college graduate with plans of pursuing a doctorate in biotechnology, said, "Yes, Paul Uncle. India has a lot of Muslims. Muslim women typically dress in black."

I got a kick out of my niece referring to me as "Paul Uncle" instead of "Uncle Paul."

Rajesh kept driving adeptly through the heavy traffic. To my left, I noticed a large fenced-in park with thick green trees. "Paulie," my wife said, "we're coming up on the university that my dad graduated from. See, to your left."

I looked to my left and saw beautiful old three-story buildings of white stone with well-manicured grounds.

"Dad graduated from that college. It was founded by the Jesuits." (He had passed away nearly a decade before).

"I see," I said. I kept observing things and taking photos with my cell phone. We passed a Christian church that had a big sign in front of it, reading, "Don't Worry About Your Life." I also saw a small sign in the back of one of the three-wheeled auto carts that read, "Life Is Safe If Driving Safe." I got a real kick out of that one.

Rajesh, who spoke a bit of English, said we were running low on gas, so he pulled into a nearby gas station. About three-fourths of the vehicles waiting to gas up were motorcycles. The gas station brand was Indian Oil, the national brand.

My wife handed some rupee notes to Rajesh, and after about a five-minute wait, he parked next to one of the gas pumps, killed the engine, and an attendant began to pump gas into our car. I noticed a motorcycle to my left with four passengers: a small boy with a gas tank between his legs; his dad, the driver, with his hands on the handlebars; and the mom, wearing a yellow sari, sitting sidesaddle and holding an infant. The mom and dad wore sandals while the child and infant were barefoot. And no one was wearing a helmet. Such a scene was ubiquitous.

Rajesh pulled out of the gas station, moving the steering wheel and shifting gears as necessary while beeping the horn, also as necessary, to get our car on a main road. The unit of measure for gas in India is liters, and knowing how much Rajesh paid for the liters of gas, I did the quick conversion using the calculator in my cell phone. It had cost the equivalent of $3.50 a gallon.

We passed many buildings, most of them old. Then my wife said, "Paulie, look to your right. See the statue in the middle of the street? That's a famous actor, and his house is also to the right."

I looked in that direction and saw a statue about ten feet in height mounted on a concrete stand of a similar height. Beyond the statue was a huge three-story home with palm trees and well-maintained grounds. I once read that actors are revered in India, and at times they enter politics as second careers.

We kept riding the narrow vehicle-crammed streets. I noticed a KFC restaurant to my left, and then, not far away, a Pizza Hut to our right. "Cool," I said. "KFC and Pizza Hut. Maybe we can do lunch there today."

"Yes, Paul Uncle," my niece replied. "We have Subway too, and there's a Domino's Pizza not too far from my grandmother's home."

Our destination was a gift shop, because my wife wanted to buy some souvenirs. Suddenly, to my left, there was a long concrete wall, about five feet in height, with a sign that read, "No Bills."

"Honey, what does 'No Bills' mean on that wall? *Bills* to me refers to money, as in monetary bills."

"It means, 'Don't paste posters on this wall.'"

"Oh, I see," I said, as I kept taking photos.

We arrived at the gift shop some five minutes later. Rajesh parked the Suzuki and waited inside it. My wife, niece, and I entered the store.

My wife and I had shopped at many Indian gift stores in the United States, but this one was considerably bigger than any I had experienced. On its three levels were tons of shelves filled with all kinds of small ornaments like tiny Ganeshas, tiny elephants, and small jewelry boxes. Most items were made of bronze, but some were made of reddish-brown wood. There were paintings, some jewelry items, and many massive statues of either Ganesha or Buddha.

In the end, my wife and niece bought a mix of items while I bought several small bowls—intricately carved and painted—for colleagues at work. When it came time to pay at the cash register, I knew to step aside and let my wife handle that task, because negotiating over prices—except at restaurants and gas stations, where prices are fixed—is expected in India, something Westerners like me are often both unfamiliar and uncomfortable with.

My wife cleverly put her negotiation skills to work to obtain discounted prices, and we paid for the items with one of the prepaid credit cards. We exited the store and hopped into the car, where Rajesh had been patiently awaiting us. I snapped on my seatbelt. Next stop was a men's fashion store. We arrived there in ten minutes.

I was fifty-fifty about buying suits, simply because I felt I had enough clothes back home. But a month earlier, another one of my wife's sisters and her two children had visited this very store, and my nephew had bought two suits of high quality at reasonable prices. Armed with this information, we agreed it would be a good idea to visit this store.

We entered the store, and right away an older women, dressed in a beautiful yellow sari, started showing us different materials of different colors. There was some back-and-forth as we viewed different samples, and I finally settled on a dark-brown material. Next came a tailor who took my measurements, and the final stop was paying for the soon-to-be-made suit. Here too I allowed my wife to do the negotiating. She finally settled on a price roughly the equivalent of two hundred dollars. A suit like it in the United States would have run me double that price.

"The suit will be ready in two days," the male cashier said.

Cool, I thought.

We exited the store and hopped into the car. Our next stop was a jewelry store my wife wanted to visit. We arrived there in about twenty minutes. Along the way, we passed various stores and apartment buildings. One store was clearly a tire shop, because rows and rows of tires lined it. The sign outside read "Tyre." *More examples of the differences in the English language*, I thought.

We entered the jewelry store, and my niece and I followed my wife to the third floor by way of a modern elevator. When we got to the third floor, they started looking at jewelry—mostly bangles and earrings. I took a seat to relax. Immediately I noticed the employees of this jewelry store—at least the ones on that floor—were all men, neatly dressed in pressed pants and collared shirts, and all of them walking barefoot on the shiny tile floors. One young employee offered me coffee, which I politely refused, since I'd quit drinking coffee a year before. I also noticed two younger employees dusting and stocking shelves. Both of these young men wore earrings. It was the first time I'd seen Indian men wearing earrings.

Suddenly the lights in the store went off. Luckily, it was sunny out, and the store wall facing the street was a huge picture window that allowed plenty of sunlight in. I remembered reading that many parts of India periodically suffer power outages, and I figured this was one of those times. Business continued, since the store was adequately lit by sunlight.

About ten minutes later, the lights came back on, and the young man who had asked if I wanted coffee offered me bottled water, which I accepted. My wife and niece kept trying out bangles, and to my left I noticed two women, one old and one young, wearing long black dresses with most of their heads covered. I figured they were Muslim. They were trying out bangles too.

We stayed at the jewelry store for at least an hour, my wife and niece settling for a few gold bangles. Surprisingly, despite my wife's best negotiating efforts, the store manager, a middle-aged man, wouldn't budge on prices.

Our next planned stop was special to me and necessitates a bit of a backstory. Three years before, around the Christmas season of 2013, I had bought an issue of *National Geographic* that was all about Jesus and his apostles. I read that issue one Sunday afternoon while my wife was preparing dinner, and toward the end of the issue was an article about St. Thomas, the apostle who doubted Jesus's resurrection and who said he needed to see Jesus's wounds from the crucifixion before he'd believe such an assertion. When Jesus appeared to him, wounds and all, Doubting Thomas, as he came to be known, no longer doubted the resurrection.

Importantly, the end of the article on St. Thomas stated something to the effect of "Thomas moved to the lands of the East, preaching the good word, performing miracles through the assistance of God, and converting the people. He died as a martyr in Madras, India, in AD 72. A chapel where he preached still stands there today."

"Honey," I said excitedly. "I'm reading about St. Thomas, one of Jesus's apostles, and it says that he died in Madras and that there's a chapel there still standing today."

"Yes, that's true," my wife said as she kept cooking rice. "There's a church in Madras for him. Madras is now called Chennai. It's a well-known church."

My niece had some errands to run, so we dropped her off at the university where she was a student. She was meeting friends to complete those errands. But before we dropped her off, we discussed our plans for lunch. "I'm in the mood for KFC and pizza," I said. "I want to check out the differences, if any, between KFC here and in the States, and whether Indian pizza is different from American pizza. We can bring the food to your mom's house." My wife agreed, and my niece said, "Paul Uncle, there is a mall not too far away. It has a KFC and a McDonald's and a Subway. Perhaps we can do pizza tonight from Domino's."

"Sounds great," I said. "We'll do pizza tonight."

Rajesh drove another block, and we dropped off my niece.

In roughly thirty minutes, Rajesh and my wife and I arrived at St. Thomas church.

Rajesh parked the car and stayed in it while my wife and I walked up the stairs to the church, which was set on a steep hill. As we walked up the concrete walkway, I noticed many stray dogs along the path, most of them medium in size and light brown. Many of the dogs lay in the middle of the stone steps. Sometimes I couldn't tell if a dog was dead or just sleeping. I also noticed many goats along the walkway. Most of them were in the low grass fields to our left and right. Some of the goats were lying next to the walkway, close enough for us to touch them.

I took photos and kept climbing the steps. I noticed an older woman, wearing a blue sari, bent down and sweeping the walkway, her broom a bunch of twigs. Stray dogs kept trotting about. I noticed an occasional depiction of one of the Stations of the Cross along the short walls that lined the walkway. Besides the older woman sweeping the walkway steps, we were the only people in sight. I looked behind me and captured the scenery: Chennai was immense—white buildings everywhere. There were great views even though it was hazy.

After about twenty minutes of walking up the numerous steps, we reached the church. It was small, made of white stone with brown trim. A few people were walking around, all Indians. I read signs and took photos. St. Thomas had preached and died there in AD 72. He apparently preached in a hut—of which there was a replica—and the church was built many centuries after his death. I took many photos and kept absorbing the sights.

We entered the church, as it was open to the public. There were a few people inside, some praying while sitting in the wooden pews, others walking around and reading framed paintings and write-ups on various saints. Photos weren't allowed, so I just walked around and read about numerous saints for ten to fifteen minutes.

We stepped out of the back of the church, and I immediately noticed a small building with a sign that read, "For Abandoned Babies." Apparently it was an orphanage, but I saw no one there, and the doors were closed.

We walked around the corner, and I saw a big statue of Mother Teresa and an even bigger one of Pope John Paul II. I took more photos. Then I noticed a small square with a black iron bench, and on the bench was a statue of a man lying as if sleeping, a blanket covering him. Above the statue of the sleeping man was a sign that read, "Homeless Jesus," and next to the bench was a metal box for donations.

We kept walking around the grounds and taking photos. To the right, next to the tall statue of Mother Teresa but a bit below the top of the hill, was a small concrete building with signs advertising various courses and a jobs program. There was also a sign for restrooms.

When we entered the small building, an older Indian woman greeted us and offered us coffee and tea. We politely declined her offer but stated that we needed to use the restroom. "Yes, of course," she said, "to the right."

After our bathroom break, we exited the small building and started walking down the walkway steps. Walking downhill was much easier than walking up, and in no more than ten minutes we were at the base of the walkway, Rajesh waiting for us in the car.

We got in, and Rajesh spun around the corner. There, to our immediate right, was yet another church, this one dedicated to St. Patrick, the patron saint of Ireland. We got out of the car, and I started taking more photos. A nativity scene was to the left of the church, and next to it was a large plastic display of Santa Claus. We took more photos, entered the church, and walked around the grounds. In fifteen minutes, we were back in the car with Rajesh, heading to the mall my niece had mentioned.

We reached the mall in about twenty minutes. Once there, Rajesh had to steer into a large parking garage and get a ticket for the mall's paid parking. He picked up the ticket and parked on the second floor of the mall. My wife and I entered the mall while Rajesh stayed in the car.

The mall had various floors and was modern in appearance. There were many stores, with most brands unfamiliar to me. There, for the first time, I saw some women—mainly teenagers—wearing pants instead of the traditional saris, but saris still dominated.

We arrived at the KFC, and right away I noticed it was a small but very clean restaurant. I looked up at the lighted menu above the cashier. *Cool*, I thought. *Halfway around the world, and I'm getting a slice of Americana.*

The menu was a lot shorter than one in a typical KFC back in the States. I didn't see mashed potatoes with gravy, for example, and there was no sign of biscuits and chicken potpie. Surprisingly, there was no Original Recipe chicken either, which is my favorite, but there was the crispy variety. And there were chicken strips with numerous sauces, including barbecue and varieties I didn't recognize.

We ordered chicken strips for us and my mother-in-law, and a chicken sandwich with rice for Rajesh. When the cashier asked, "For here or for take-away," I hesitated a slight moment and quickly figured "take-away" meant "take-out."

"For take-away," I said.

Next stop, sixty feet away, was the McDonald's in the mall, which was also small and very clean. There, too, the menu was limited from an American perspective—not a single beef-based burger. There were soft drinks and a fish sandwich, the latter of which we ordered for my mother-in-law. Dominating the menu were chicken and a sandwich called the McAllo: the plain McAllo Tikki sandwich, the Mexican McAllo Tikki sandwich, and the Lebanese McAllo Tikki sandwich. The menu also featured the Big Spicy Paneer wrap, the Veg Maharaja Mac, and the Chicken Maharaja Mac. And best of all, it had McDonald's famous french fries. *Yes!*

Along with the fish fillet sandwich, we ordered fries and Cokes (I wasn't in the most experimental mood), and we decided to bypass food from Subway since we'd already ordered plenty.

We paid for the food, got back in the car, paid for the parking, picked up my niece, and in forty minutes we were at my mother-in-law's house eating a combination of Indian food (*chapatis* and rice) and American fast-food (chicken strips, fish fillet, and french fries).

After lunch, we relaxed, chitchatted, and watched Indian television, which featured news and old musicals. Our plan for the evening was to visit the second church dedicated to St. Thomas and then Chennai's beach on the shores of the Bay of Bengal.

Rajesh drove us to the church, which was in the same direction as the beach. I sat in the usual front passenger's seat with seatbelt fastened, while my wife and niece took the back seats, which had nonfunctioning seat belts. The ride to the church was about thirty minutes. By then, the sights of cows and goats and families of four on motorcycles were familiar, as was the constant sound of beeping vehicles.

The second church dedicated to St. Thomas was substantially larger than the one we'd visited earlier in the day. It was where St. Thomas was interred. There were more visitors at this church, and almost all were Indians.

We took exterior photos of the large church, which was white stone; photos weren't allowed inside. We walked in and saw different statues of different saints, but St. Thomas's statue was by far the largest and most prominent. It was near the front of the altar, next to Jesus on the cross.

Near the front entrance was a desk filled with brochures, and next to the desk was a sign pointing downstairs, where St. Thomas was interred. We followed the signs, went downstairs, and followed more signs to the internment site. After walking nearly one hundred feet, we saw a life-size replica of St. Thomas encased in a transparent glass box, lying down on its back. It appeared to be made of plastic. There was a small wooden pew next to it, and a middle-aged Indian man was kneeling in that pew, praying.

We exited the church and linked up with Rajesh, who was waiting for us in the car. He removed his sandals, put the car in gear, and sped off onto a main road. Some ten minutes later, we were parked at Chennai Beach.

Chennai Beach is the widest beach I've ever seen. The distance from the long, narrow parking lot, where many motorcycles and motor scooters were parked, to the waterline had to be four hundred feet, all of it soft, thick, gray sand. There were many people on the beach even as dusk was setting in. (Chennai sunrises and sunsets always occur at six thirty, morning and evening). I saw a woman ride a white horse as well as a Ferris wheel, small kids enjoying themselves, and a woman cooking ears of corn on an open fire. Some young children tried to sell us some sort of pamphlet.

As we walked close to the seashore, I saw that the Bay of Bengal's waters were rough with sizable waves. There was a strong breeze and a fair amount of paper trash scattered on the beach. I saw no bathing suits or bikinis; there, too, women wore saris or the traditional salwar kameez. I saw only three swimmers, all men.

We turned around and headed back to the car, enjoying the sea breeze along the way. When we got there, Rajesh took my wife and me back to the hotel. He then took my niece back to my mother-in-law's house, parked the car there, and headed back to his nearby home.

Once at the hotel, we dropped off our bags in our room, and I decided to check out the hotel's bar, named Bike and Barrel. My wife accompanied me to the bar, which was on the third floor. We sat on bar stools, and I ordered a Stella Artois draft beer. Michael Jackson and Bon Jovi hits were playing, and I noticed that all the patrons were Indian men and a few Indian women, plus two Chinese women. As in the downstairs buffet room, a *Casablanca* poster hung prominently on a wall.

I drank the beer, and then we went back to our room. I changed into shorts and a T-shirt, and I decided to check the contents of the desk to the right of the flat-screen television. I opened its sole drawer and saw a Bible and a copy of the *Bhagavad Gita*, one of Hinduism's most important texts. I decided to lie on the bed, and I started flipping pages and skimming through the book, the central teaching of which is the attainment of freedom by performing one's duty in life.

I then started thinking about our plans for tomorrow, which was visiting the historical sites at Mahabalipuram, about a two-hour drive from Chennai. I slept well.

Day three started with a hearty breakfast in the hotel's buffet room. After breakfast, my wife and I met my niece and Rajesh in my mother-in-law's car. After thirty minutes of city driving, we reached the outskirts of Chennai, where we got on a highway and followed the shores of the Bay of Bengal, heading south. Along the way, I saw more modernity than in Chennai proper: big glass buildings that were either large medical clinics or technology centers, an aboveground train system that resembled Washington DC's Metro, and large modern buses that resembled Greyhounds.

Once we got on the highway—a highway that had dividing lines painted on it—I estimated that Rajesh reached speeds of about sixty miles an hour, zipping along, passing similar but slower cars. I saw a nice condo development to our right that was adjacent to a small interior bay, and I saw cows both along the edge of the highway and in beautiful green pastures far from the highway. There were fewer motorcycles and motor scooters than in the streets of Chennai, and the sight of green pastures with thick trees, including palm trees, was a nice break from the traffic, tall buildings, and ever-present beeps of horns on the Chennai streets. In two hours, we reached Mahabalipuram. Our first stop was Shore Temple.

Short Temple is a UNESCO World Heritage site, and for good reasons. The beautiful, intricate temple, carved from granite, was completed in the seventh century. A square, lined with detailed and lifelike carvings of cows, encircles the two pyramid shapes that comprise Shore Temple. Apparently there were seven similar temples, but the ravages of the nearby Bay of Bengal washed those away.

I couldn't help but feel like Indiana Jones when viewing and photographing those beautiful structures. The main take-away was clear to me: India is an old country that takes its religion seriously.

My niece told me that most of the visitors came from other parts of India, and that's when I noticed numerous large buses and student groups, supporting her point. I also saw some foreign tourists—Caucasians and a few Asians—walking around with cameras around their necks, wearing large Panama hats to block the sun's rays. But Indians were by far the largest group of visitors.

Shops selling hats, bottled water, coconuts and coconut water, and various souvenirs lined the lot where the buses were parked. I saw beggars, too, sitting with their legs crossed Indian-style, asking for food or money. There, too, the beggars were either older men or older women; there were no child beggars. I bought a Panama hat for shade.

After Shore Temple, Rajesh took us to another site in Mahabalipuram, and my niece served as our guide. We saw massive granite carvings of life-size elephants that looked real. *Absolutely amazing*, I kept thinking.

Around noon, we headed back toward Chennai, the game plan being to stop for lunch at a seaside resort. As we were driving north toward the resort, I noticed a field where teenage boys were playing cricket. I told Rajesh to stop the car so I could take photos of the match. I had always wanted to see a cricket match, and there was my chance. I watched a few batsmen and took some photos.

We arrived at the resort about an hour after leaving the cricket field. Like at our hotel, security was tight; guards checked the trunk and underbody of our car for bombs. Rajesh dropped us off, and we gave him money to get more gas and his lunch. We figured we'd be at the resort for no more than two hours.

We entered the resort, and standing next to a large Christmas tree in the corner of the lobby was a large plastic Santa Claus. The air-conditioning felt great, and a well-stocked bar stood in the corner opposite the Christmas tree. Beyond the bar was a hallway that led to a large buffet room surrounded by picture windows. A walkway to the right of the bar led to the outdoor portion of the resort.

My wife, niece, and I walked down the outdoor walkway to check out the seafood restaurant near the beach. Along the way we saw a beautiful swimming pool, well-manicured grounds, and an outdoor bar with a roof made of straw. Adults and kids were swimming, and a small bar was right at the edge of the pool, its patrons sipping drinks as they sat in the water. Some women wore bikinis, and there were foreigners, mostly white Europeans. But most of the patrons were Indians.

The menu of the seaside restaurant looked appetizing, but we decided to eat lunch in the buffet room to take advantage of the air-conditioning, even though there was a pleasant sea breeze. The buffet's excellent menu was a mix of Western and Indian cuisine. I remember eating a tasty garlic chicken dish. I also had a beer, a glass of wine, and two servings of chocolate mousse from the dessert bar. As I was eating, I noticed that all the servants were male. Our bill, for three people, came to the equivalent of forty dollars. In the States, such a lunch would have easily been triple the cost.

After lunch, Rajesh took us back to Chennai, which was about an hour's drive. We hung out at my mother-in-law's house, watched some TV, and decided to get some take-away food. We settled on Chinese and Indian as well as Domino's pizza. I had two slices of pizza, which had tiny pieces of chicken on them. (My niece had told me pepperoni wasn't available.) Though it was considerably different from American pizza, mostly because it had goat cheese instead of mozzarella, I liked the Indian pizza slices.

After dinner, Rajesh brought my wife and I back to our hotel. I went to the Bike and Barrel again, had a drink, and settled in for the night in our hotel room. The game plan for the next day was to visit Pondicherry, a former French colonial settlement three hours south of Chennai.

The next morning, I showered and shaved, and began reading complementary copies of the *Chennai Times*, the local paper, in English. It had a large entertainment section (actors are revered in India), and cricket dominated the sport pages. In the political section, the focus was corruption. There were also crime stories (one man had thrown kerosene on his wife and lit a match, burning her to death). And the key economic story was that of "note bank," the ban on certain currency notes to help curb corruption. I found out George Michael and Carrie Fisher had both died (too young, in my opinion), and that more than 40 percent of Indians didn't have access to the Internet. There also were major train derailments somewhere in India, making me wonder if I'd ever trust that mode of transportation in India.

My wife and I had breakfast at the hotel, then we got into the Suzuki car—Rajesh and one of my sisters-in-law were waiting for us. It was a hot, sunny, humid day with hazy skies. Rajesh, driving barefoot as always, quickly got us out of the Chennai traffic by beeping and maneuvering through the streets. In about fifteen minutes, we found ourselves on the nice highway we'd taken the day before. I noted some of the beautiful buildings we had driven by the previous day: hospitals and medical clinics, the massive aboveground metro train, and modern buildings made of steel and glass, housing IT and biotech companies.

About an hour into our three-hour drive, I saw the aftermath of the only car accident I would see in India—a small car heavily dented on the driver's side and with a cracked windshield. Two police officers were at the scene, and the small police cruiser was flashing its blue lights. Fortunately, no one was hurt, at least from what I could tell.

We slowly passed the accident and proceeded to our destination, and like the day before, I saw the beautiful green pastures, cows grazing on them, thick green brush, big trees that resembled oaks, palm trees aplenty, goats standing along the streets, some cows lying on the side of the road near the highway, an occasional beggar (always an older person), and the ever-present waves of the Bay of Bengal, always to our left, which meant we were heading south. At one point we came across huge salt paddies to our right, which resembled fine white-sand beaches, surrounded by a receding lake. I had never seen salt paddies, and I made sure to take lots of photos.

Shortly after passing the salt paddies, Rajesh slowed the car, and we got into a queue to a toll booth ahead. We paid our toll (I forget the amount) and proceeded to Pondicherry, which was only ten minutes away.

Indian people settled the areas of Pondicherry many centuries ago, but in 1674 the French made it the headquarters of the French East India Company. India was a British colony for three centuries until it was granted independence after the Second World War, but other European powers also claimed lands on the Indian subcontinent. Britain dominated, but the Portuguese, Dutch, and French had their footprints in India, with the French basing their presence in this coastal city, population 650,000. The European powers came to India for spices, trade, power, and money, and to convert the inhabitants to Christianity.

The French legacy in Pondicherry is preserved in its French quarter, which consists of a few blocks where huge, beige colonial buildings and tree-lined streets dominate. We reached the French quarter after about twenty minutes of driving in hectic and crowded traffic just like that in Chennai. It was lunchtime, and we settled on a restaurant recommended to us by one of my wife's sisters, who had visited there with her husband and two daughters in early August.

We entered the restaurant, which also served as a hotel, and sat in the open court portion. There we could see the various stories of the hotel, all from the inside. Beautiful palm trees stood at the corners of the open court. Looking straight out, I could see a light-blue sky sprinkled with puffy white clouds. It was a beautiful afternoon, and the tables were quickly filling up.

I noticed a balance of European and American tourists together with Indian patrons. A young French-speaking couple was sitting at a table next to ours, drinking Budweiser.

I ordered chicken tikka masala and a glass of red wine while my wife and sister-in-law ordered rice dishes. The service was slow, but the scenery was beautiful, and the food, once it finally arrived, was excellent. We topped our lunches with two excellent desserts, one a chocolate cake and the other a mango pie.

After lunch, my wife, sister-in-law, and I walked a couple of blocks to an immense stone building housing a large bookstore. Rajesh had lunch at another locale and waited for us in the car. Tall wooden bookshelves lined the walls nearly up to the ceiling and were filled to the brim with books. There were only two other patrons there. On the concrete floor were three aisles with shorter wooden bookshelves, about four feet in height. I walked the aisles and noticed books in Hindi, English, and French. As I made my way to the front entrance (we had entered by the back door), I saw bigger hardcover books, all used, prominently displayed. I recognized a few David Baldacci best sellers, but the other titles I didn't recognize.

We stayed about thirty minutes, checking out books and their titles, but we didn't make any purchases. Rajesh picked us up, and we decided to check out Pondicherry's beach.

After about ten minutes of crowded city driving, we reached a beautiful boulevard running parallel to Pondicherry's Bay of Bengal shoreline. I asked Rajesh to stop and park the car so we could check out the beach. He did, and we got out of the car. (I saw no parking meters.) The beach was only a tenth of the width of Chennai Beach. Huge, bright black boulders lined the beach right up to the ocean's edge. These boulders were jagged and about five feet high by five feet wide. I saw only a few people walking on them, gingerly navigating their way from one boulder to another. No one was swimming in the choppy waves; instead, people were walking on the gray sand next to the boulevard. I took photos and enjoyed the sun mixed with the ocean breeze.

Next we decided to take a boat ride at a nearby lake— another recommendation from my sister-in-law, who had visited Pondicherry in the summer. Rajesh knew exactly how to get there: we stayed on the ocean boulevard for about ten minutes, then got on city streets and made our way to a main drive. Along the way, we saw a huge statue of Gandhi on Pondicherry Beach. I took photos of the statue while in the car. The lake was about fifteen minutes from the statue.

Rajesh parked the car, and my wife, sister-in-law, and I got in line to purchase tickets for the boat ride. The line was very long, so my sister-in-law insisted she stay in line and purchase the tickets while we waited next to the entrance gate, which was under the cover of big trees. We agreed to her plan and quickly got into the shade.

While we waited for her and the tickets, I noticed two things: patience and coconuts. As Indians patiently waited to buy tickets, I witnessed no complaints, no arguments, no expressions of frustration. I did see young children running about, here and there, being a bit antsy, but their parents—whether the mom or dad—were quick to get them back in the fold, quiet and in order. Such a long line in the hot sun, and the fact that it didn't move very fast, would have brought complaints in the United States, like "Hey, why don't you hire more employees to get this line moving" and "This is ridiculous."

My second observation was of an older woman, dressed in a sari, sitting on the floor next to the shaded gate where we stood. She was chopping the tips off green coconuts with a large machete and pushing a straw into the openings for patrons to drink from. She chopped a coconut in one or two chops, disposed of the sliced edge on the side of the asphalt road, stuck a straw in, and then made a monetary transaction with the waiting patron. Business was brisk, and the old woman had her routine down: chop, dispose of chopped edge, stick in a straw, make change, next customer.

I'm not a fan of coconut, so I decided not to try the drink, but it was fun to observe her. I also noticed the coconuts didn't have the rough, brown exteriors we're used to, but instead were light green and smooth to the touch.

After waiting about thirty minutes (luckily in the shade), there was still no sign of my sister-in-law with the tickets. We decided to abandon our plan and visit another restaurant for drinks and a bathroom break. My wife and I went back to the line, found her sister, and told her of our revised plans. She agreed, and Rajesh drove us to a small, quiet restaurant in Pondicherry.

The restaurant was on the second floor of a big square building. Inside was a family of five at a corner table. My wife, sister-in-law, and I sat at the other end of the restaurant, next to the entrance that led to an outdoor, unshaded patio. Occupying a small table at the center of the patio were two young white women drinking sodas and smoking cigarettes, their nearly empty dishes to the sides of their table.

We sat at the table near the patio entrance, ordered drinks (juices and water), and took bathroom breaks. The interior pitched roof was made of bamboo, and a large goldfish tank occupied a raised table next to the bar area behind us. We stayed at this quiet restaurant for about forty-five minutes before we decided to head back to Chennai.

Rajesh picked us up and started maneuvering his way out of the narrow motorcycle-filled streets of Pondicherry. In no time, we came upon a city circle, and Rajesh carefully negotiated the circle like the other vehicles, without the aid of driving lanes and signs, because there weren't any. After the circle, we got on a narrow street, and I noticed a large crowd had formed toward the middle of the straightaway road. I forget if it was I or someone else in our car who noticed the large decorated elephant that had drawn the crowd. I thought, *Cool. I'm in India, and I always wanted to see an elephant, and here's my chance.* I asked Rajesh to stop the car.

My wife and sister-in-law and I got out of the car and quickly joined the crowd of onlookers. We made our way to the front, and I started taking photos. I was amazed just how huge the animal was. A slight man sat atop it, right behind its massive ears, while another man sat on a stool between the elephant's left legs. A semicircle of onlookers had formed in front of the elephant, and I noticed bright-colored designs on the elephant's forehead and around its eyes. We got close to the front semicircle line, and I kept taking photos.

"The people in the front line are receiving blessings from the elephant," my wife informed me. Then I noticed that whenever a patron stepped forward, the man sitting on the stool gave short soft taps to the elephant's front left leg while the man atop the elephant guided the elephant's head and trunk toward the patron. The elephant raised his trunk and gently tapped the top of the patron's head with the tip of his trunk. On it went like this, a patron stepping forward and the elephant gently tapping the patron's head.

Sometime back, my wife had told me that an elephant with a raised trunk is a sign of good luck, and I was witnessing that, because the elephant's trunk was almost always raised, going from left to right, right to left, tapping the tops of patrons' heads. Some patrons fed the elephant—peanuts, I think—and then immediately received its blessing. My sister-in-law got a blessing, but I decided to stay on the sidelines and take photos. It was all fun and enjoyable to watch.

We hopped back in the car and started our long drive back to Chennai. Along the way I noticed plenty of cows along the highway, some slowly walking, others sitting and asleep. I also noticed small trucks, usually white, their beds filled with thick yellow-brown branches ten feet in length.

When I inquired what they were, my sister-in-law said they were recently harvested sugarcanes.

Dusk quickly settled in, and it was dark around six, but the traffic moved steadily. Once we reached the outskirts of Chennai, my wife insisted we have dinner at a popular South Indian restaurant right off the highway. We stopped at the restaurant, entered it, and quickly found a booth to sit in. We placed our orders—rice dishes and dosas, both delicious.

At this restaurant, I had the pleasant experience of having Rajesh join us for a meal. Though he sat in the booth next to ours, it was nice to have him with us. It had been hard not to wonder why he wasn't eating with us on previous occasions, but I said nothing. I'm a big believer in "when in Rome, do as the Romans." Bottom line, it was nice to have Rajesh share that one meal with us.

We arrived at our hotel around nine, and I called it a day.

The next day was our last in Chennai, given that our flight was booked for early the next morning. My wife, sister-in-law, and I spent the morning doing a bit of shopping and picked up my tailored suit. Lunch was special, for it took place at a renowned popular restaurant that usually required reservations. It was a late lunch that we started at about two in the afternoon. Beautiful hand-carved crown molding lined the ceiling seams, and ornate bronze statues of Ganesha were placed in the corners of the large upscale restaurant.

The cuisine was South Indian, and I remember receiving at least five courses. Our plates were lined with bright-green banana leaves, and the waiters (all men) kept bringing us various rice dishes and tasty vegetables. It was a delicious meal, complete with a mango rice pudding for dessert. Our lunch lasted nearly three hours.

The rest of the day was spent at my mother-in-law's house. We relaxed, watched television, and exchanged gifts. And we paid Rajesh for his much-needed driving services.

Our taxi arrived on time the next morning and took us to the airport. We got our luggage out, paid the cab driver, and said goodbye to my sister-in-law. While waiting in the long line for the customs officers to check our passports and flight reservations, I began to reflect on the last few days I'd spent in that part of India. The sheer amount of traffic and the form it came in (tons of motorcycles and motor scooters) will be a lasting memory, as will the constant beeping of so many vehicles.

As for surprises during our trip, there were many: the fact that many of the scooter drivers were women, and that they wore saris while driving; the fact that I saw only the aftermath of one accident; and the treatment of dogs—really the maltreatment of them (no owners, no petting, no feeding, all strays).

I saw slums in Chennai, but I thought I'd see more, and I thought they'd be bigger and occupy more land. As for beggars, I saw some, and it's always sad to see people struggling, but given what I'd read about India and the footage I'd seen about India on television, I thought I'd see more beggars. I'm glad I didn't.

One of the biggest surprises about Chennai, second only

to the traffic and its format, was the Christian influence I saw: a good number of churches and chapels; schools named after saints; many pictures of Jesus, including on the back of three-wheeled auto carts; and displays of Santa Claus—good old St. Nick himself—in a fair number of stores, restaurants, and our hotel. I saw more Hindu temples than Christian churches, but I saw more Christian churches than mosques, though Muslims far outnumber Christians in India.

People walking barefoot was a surprise (but not a big surprise, as most people wore sandals), as was the fact that there were a few differences in the English language: "Paul Uncle" not "Uncle Paul"; "make way" rather than "yield"; "take-away instead of "take-out"; "Do Not Place Bills Here" instead of "Do Not Place Posters Here"— showing that every English-speaking country has its own spin on the language.

And then there were the things I didn't see. I didn't see people smoking, nor did I see people laughing. Public displays of affection—husband and wife or boyfriend and girlfriend holding hands, kissing, or hugging in public—were nonexistent.

There wasn't a lot of laughter in public. One time we heard loud laughs coming from outside a gift store we were in, prompting us to wonder who was laughing so hard. We peeked out the store's front door to see a group of six women, all white, together with a female Indian guide, laughing. When we reentered the store, we heard one of the store's employees say dismissively, "Just a bunch of tourists, laughing."

In no way am I suggesting Indians don't laugh. When

my wife and I were relaxing and watching television at my mothers-in-law's house, there was plenty of laughing going on. But in public I didn't witness laughter except when the elephant was giving blessings in Pondicherry.

After going through the long line at the airport and finally boarding our plane, I thought of the more than three hundred photos I'd taken and whether there was one that best represented our visit to Chennai. The one photo I kept thinking of was from our visit to the ancient sites around Shore Temple. It's a photo of a modern bus parked on a side street in front of a temple, and in front of the bus a cow is resting. The temple and cow represent the importance of religion in Indian society, and the bus represents modernity in the emerging market that is India.

I enjoyed Chennai, and my wife and I plan to go back there and to other parts of India someday. Bombay and Goa and New Delhi and the Taj Mahal definitely come to mind. I'm confident there will be much to observe and experience during these future trips, and I'm looking forward to writing about them.

Printed in the United States
By Bookmasters